Glacier National Park
Attractions & Sights to See

Billy Grinslott & Kinsey Marie Books

ISBN - 9781960612939

There are many sights to see in Glacier National Park. We have listed the most popular ones. Avalanche lake is about a 5 mile hike roundtrip. It got its name because in the winter the snow does not rest well on the steep slopes of Sperry Glacier and it falls off. The Glacier behind Avalanche lake is Sperry Glacier.

Waterton Lakes National Park in Alberta, Canada was combined with the Glacier National Park to form the world's first International Peace Park. Situated on the border between the two countries and offering outstanding scenery, the park is exceptionally rich in prairie, forest, and alpine and glacial features.

Swift current Mountain trail and Swift current Lake. Remarkably maintained with awe-inspiring views, the Swift current Pass Trail is a favorite among those who frequent Glacier National Park. The hike involves a gradual ascent followed by a steep final mile to the summit, where a fire tower is located. Proceed cautiously on this 16.6-mile out-and-back trail generally considered a highly challenging route. It has awesome views and you might see a moose on this trail.

The Garden wall trail runs along the side of garden wall. The Garden Wall is a stunning glacial landform known for its array of vibrant greenery and wildflowers during summer months. Offering several hiking trails, with breathtaking views, and ample opportunity to view wildlife. The Garden Wall is a geologic ridge that was formed by glaciers as they moved across the landscape. Proceed cautiously along this 15-mile out-and-back trail

Baring Falls is a 25-30ft waterfall that can be accessed by a nearly 1-mile round-trip hike from the Sunrift Gorge off the Going to the Sun Road in Glacier National Park. Generally considered an easy route. The parking lot is located off the going to the sun road.

The 3.6-mile round-trip hike to the Red Rock Falls is a must if you are visiting the area. It is a moderate hike with plenty of scenery and views. The views at the arrival to the falls are quite impressive. A great place to take pictures. Red Rock Falls is an easy trail to a waterfall cascading down red rocks. It's also a great spot to see wildlife.

Lake Josephine is a backcountry lake despite its proximity to general amenities. This is because you cannot access it by vehicle. It's a hike-in and boat-in only access. It's a 1.2-mile hike from the Grinnell Glacier Trailhead, or you can cut that down to 0.2 miles by taking charter boats across the lake from the Many Glaciers Hotel. It provides awesome glacier views and watersports opportunities.

The hike to Cracker Lake offers a lot of scenery. It passes through wooded areas, across streams, around other lakes and some open areas with great views. Overall, the Cracker Lake Trail is a fairly moderate hike, despite its long 13 mile roundtrip distance from Many Glacier parking lot.

Jackson Glacier Overlook is home to the best view of a glacier along Going to the Sun Road, telling one of the park's most important stories. You can see Jackson Glacier from the parking area, or hike towards it along the trail to Gunsight Lake, which begins at Jackson Glacier Overlook. The Jackson Glacier Overlook is a must-see stop. Jackson Glacier is the 4th tallest mountain in Glacier National Park.

Siyeh Pass. This hike features incredible alpine meadows and great glacier views. The trail is in the trees for the first several miles. Then the trail breaks off to the east and heads up Preston Park. This is one of the prettiest alpine meadows and is a perfect spot for lunch. Mt. Siyeh is one of six peaks in Glacier park that is over 10,000 feet high, it dominates the view to the north. Sieyh pass trail is a 9 miles long hike. Generally considered a challenging route.

The Middle Fork of the Flathead River originates in the Bob Marshall Wilderness. The upper section offers recreation in a wilderness setting. Most river float trips start from Schafer Meadows, which can be reached by trail or by aircraft. The float season normally lasts from mid-May through mid-July, with peak runoff in late May. Numerous rapids can make the trip extremely difficult during peak flows. The lower section of the river offers more suitable recreation in a more developed setting.

Kintla Lake is surrounded by towering mountains and is over 8 miles in length and up to a mile wide. It is the fourth largest lake in the park. For those who canoe and kayak, it is a paddler's paradise. Fisherman will also enjoy the lake for the trout found in it. If you like to hike, pack your boots. Day hikes and trips into the backcountry can be found near the campground. Due to its remote location, the campground is very quiet and is very rarely filled, offering campers a sense of solitude. This 12.8-mile out-and-back trail is considered a moderately challenging route.

The hike to Piegan Pass is very popular for those who love hiking in mountainous areas. The view the entire way is wonderful, which makes this hike worth the effort. The Piegan Pass Trail climbs 1,670 vertical feet, which is an average amount, especially with a mountain pass involved. Piegan Pass is 7,560 feet above sea level, allowing for terrific views all around. Proceed cautiously on this 16.0-mile trail Generally considered a highly challenging route.

Hiking to Bullhead Lake is a beautiful hike in the Many Glaciers area of the Glacier National Park. The 8-mile-round-trip hike to Bullhead Lake begins near the parking lot at the Swiftcurrent Motor Inn. Generally considered a moderately challenging route. Bullhead Lake is located at the foot of the Continental Divide. Bullhead Lake is in a stunning setting. The mountains soar far above the lake, providing a beautiful location to spend some time eating lunch or fishing.

John's Lake Loop. Head out on this 2-mile loop trail generally considered an easy route. This nice hike near Lake Mc Donald passes John's Lake and then wanders by Sacred Dancing Cascade and McDonald Falls along McDonald Creek. Great hike for families or anyone looking for an easy stroll near the Lake McDonald Lodge.

Clements Mountain is located less than one mile west of the Visitor Center at Logan Pass. Clements Mt. exhibits a classic Matterhorn shape. Clements Mountain stands 8,760 feet above sea level. It is easily seen from the roadway at Logan Pass. It is in the top 5 for most photographed mountains in Glacier Park. You can also take a short hike to reach the base.

Granite Park Chalet is accessible only by foot. There are two trails to access the Granite Park Chalet. For both trails we recommend parking at the West Glacier-Agar Transit Center and taking a free Glacier National Park shuttle to the trailheads. Option 1: The Highline Trail is 7.6 miles with moderate difficulty to the chalet. Option 2: The Loop Trail is the shortest route but has a 2,300-foot climb. Spend a night and enjoy awesome views of the surrounding mountains or hike the nearby trails.

Goat Lick Overlook is a quite wildlife hot spot located right off Hwy 2, about 2.5 miles East of the Walton Ranger Station. The best time of year to see wildlife is from April to August. The mountain goats love this area because the river is full of nutrients like calcium, potassium, and magnesium, that helps replace the elements the goats typically lose from their bones during the winter months.

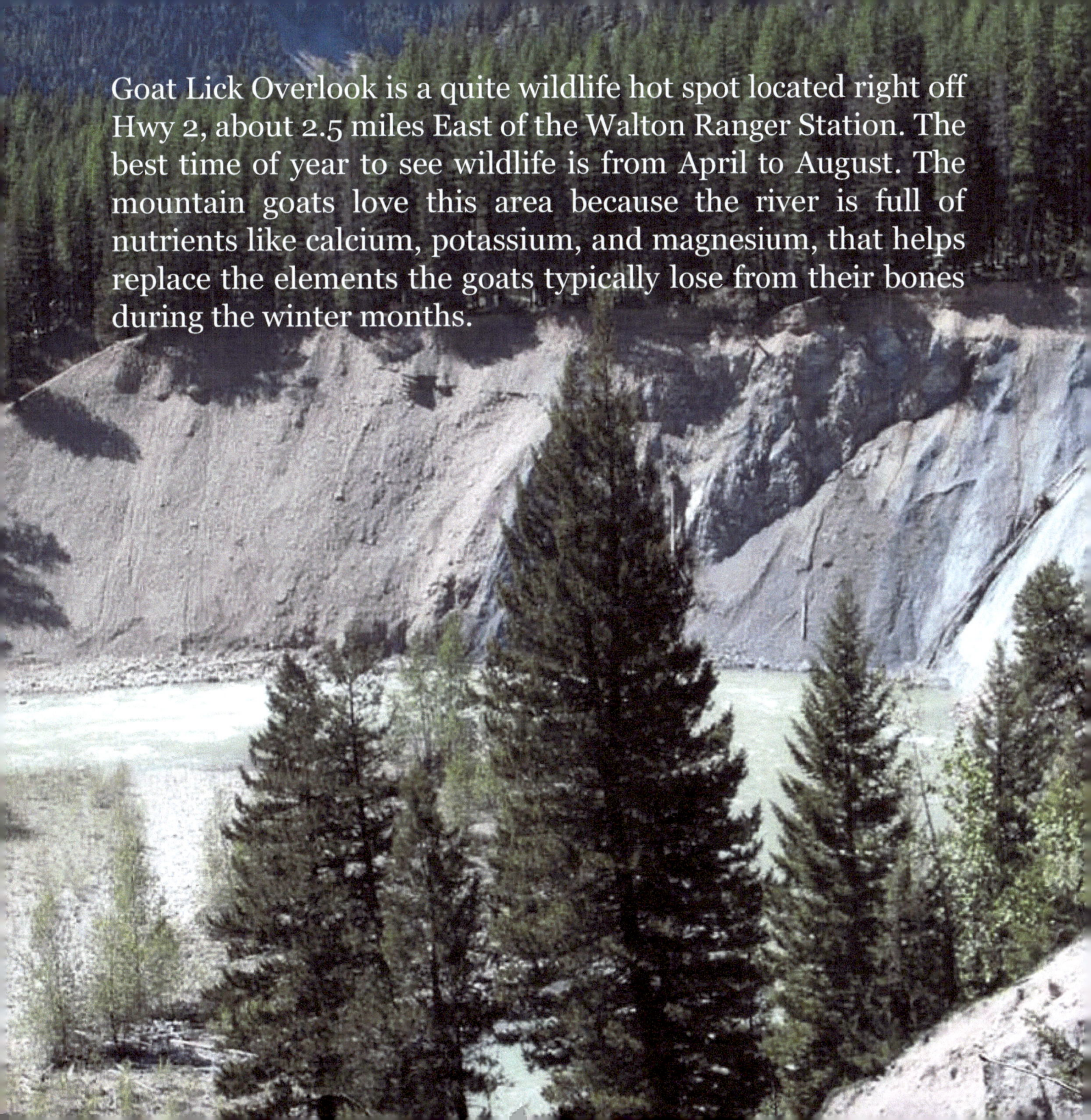

Goat Haunt is one of the park's more remote and tranquil locations. It offers opportunities to explore Glacier away from the crowds. Visitors to Goat Haunt arriving by boat only may offload at the dock and explore the exhibits at the International Peace Park shelter and walk along the paved pathway to the Ranger Station and enjoy awesome views.

The Belly River Trail takes you into the remote Belly River Valley, which is an extremely scenic region of Glacier Park. Where you can view the lake and the surrounding mountains. Backpacking in the Belly River area makes for an incredible experience. This 15-mile out-and-back trail is generally considered a moderately challenging route.

Bowman Lake is in the Northwestern corner of Glacier National Park. You can get to it by driving a couple different routes. Bowman Lake is the 3rd largest lake in Glacier National Park. It's about a mile wide and stretches 8 miles long. Bowman Lake gets its water entirely by snowmelt therefore it is a very cold lake. Bowman Lake is crystal clear. The deepest point in the lake is 253 feet deep.

Fisher cap lake is a short walk from the parking lot. It has less than a mile long loop near the lake. You can hike it in around 15 to 20 minutes. It is an easy trail to walk on. You might want to plan to spend more time around the lake. They say it's a good place to see moose. Hiking to Fisher cap Lake is worth it. The hike itself is short with almost zero elevation gain. The views at the end are quite beautiful and worth it.

The Flathead River originates in the Rocky Mountains and flows through Glacier National. Due to its protection by wilderness on both sides. It offers solitude and a peaceful quite place to get away from it all. Some people like to canoe, or river raft the river.

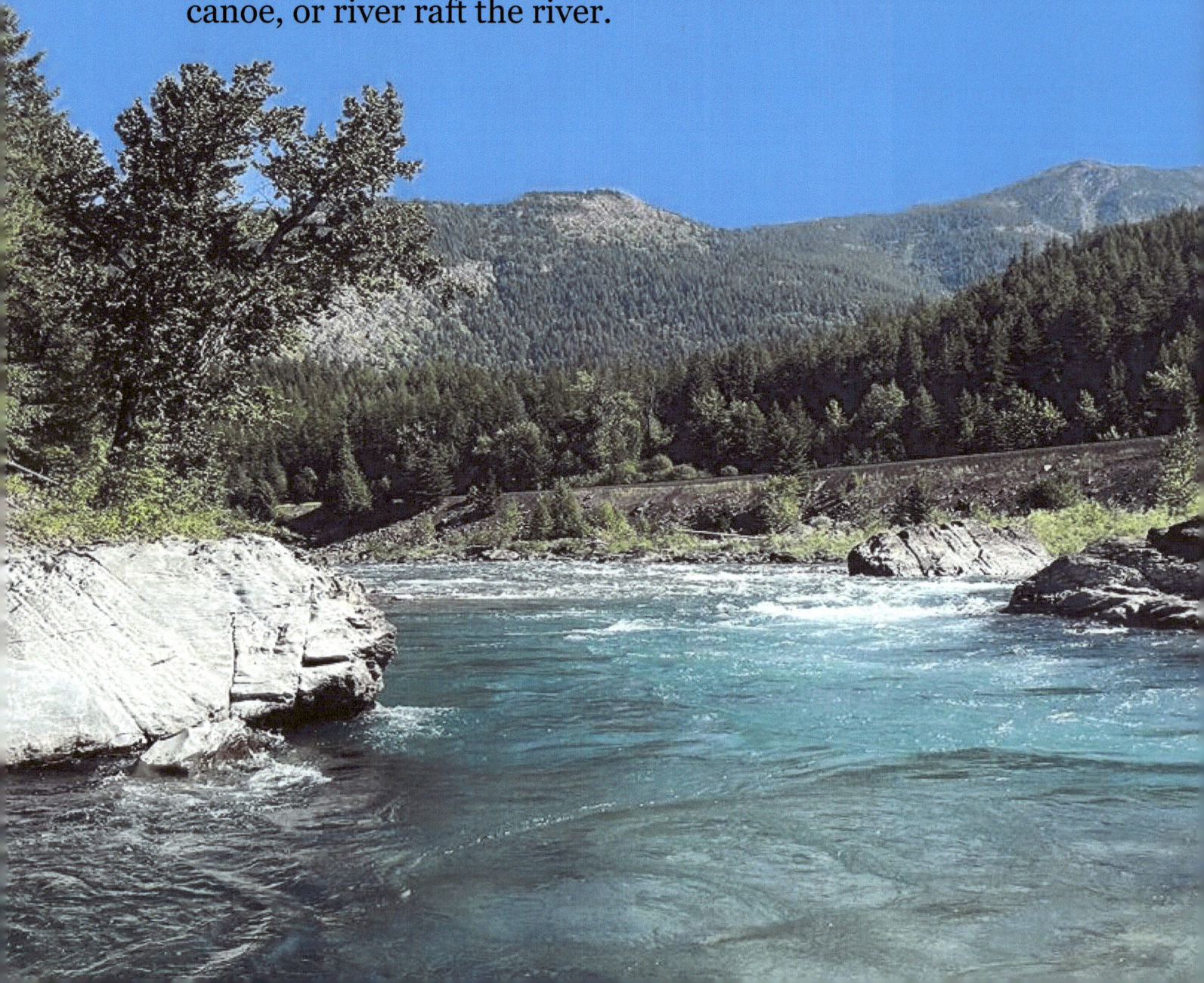

The Glacier Crest Trail is a 8 mile roundtrip hiking route in Glacier National Park. It offers awesome views over the rugged mountains and the nearby Illecillewaet Glacier. Hike up the steep incline and winding switchbacks along the trail to arrive at the end of the trail. From which point a further 300 foot trek will bring you to an amazing vantage point overlooking the glacier. This trail is both a great workout and an opportunity to experience some beautiful BC terrain.

Getting to Grinnell Glacier is challenging hike that offers something for everyone, glaciers, waterfalls, lakes, forest, wildlife, and incredible views. This 10 mile roundtrip trail is considered a challenging route. It takes an average of 5 hours to complete. This is a very popular area, so you will encounter other people. You will need to leave the dogs at home, because dogs are not allowed on this trail.

To get to Hidden Lake, it is a 5-mile roundtrip hiking trail in Montana. Generally considered a moderately challenging route, it takes an average of 3 hours to complete. This trail offers stunning views and wildlife encounters, such as mountain goats and bighorn sheep. The trail can be wet and steep in places. Trekking poles are recommended for stability.

The Highline Trail is a 15-mile roundtrip trail near Siyeh Bend, Montana. Generally considered a challenging route, it takes an average of 7 hours minimum to complete. This is a very popular area for backpacking, camping, hiking, and seeing wildlife. The trail is described as not too difficult, safe, and even enjoyable for beginners. The glacier overlook can be steep, it has great views, but be prepared.

To get to Iceberg Lake it is a 9.6-mile roundtrip trail. It takes an average of 5 hours to complete. This is a very popular area for hiking. It got its name because ice that resemble icebergs float around on the lake most of the year. The Iceberg Lake Trail has some sections. The trail has some loose rocks as well as larger rocks. Hiking shoes and poles will help you make it to the lake as easily and safely as possible.

Lake McDonald is the largest lake in Glacier National Park. It is 9.4 miles long and 1.5 miles wide, and 464 feet deep. This lake was formed from the glaciers carving their way through the earth. The trail runs alongside of the lake and has awesome views. You can also take a boat ride on the lake for better views of the scenery.

Logan Pass is reachable by car in the park. It is extremely popular with visitors. The parking lot is generally full between 8 am and 4 pm. Consider visiting this destination by using the free shuttles to avoid limited parking. Early morning light on the mountains provides excellent photographs and the chances to see wildlife are greater before the crowds arrive. You can also hike two of the area's most popular trails, the Hidden Lake trail and the Highline trail.

The trail to Running Eagle falls is a wide and a well maintained path suitable for everyone in the family. It's also one of two trails in the park that's handicap accessible. It is also a short trail that is less than a mile long. Easy to walk and has great views.

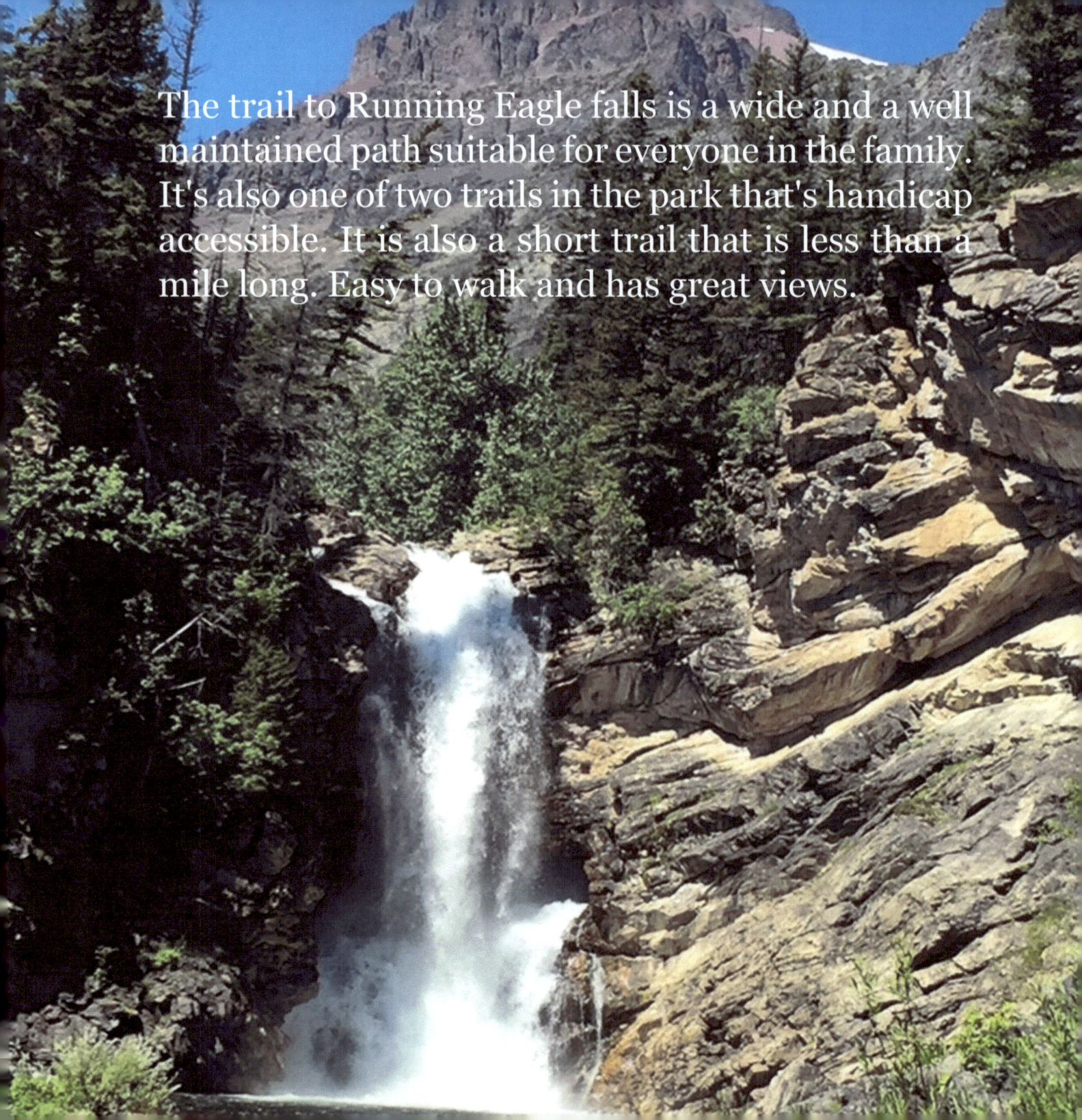

The Trail of the Cedars is one of two wheelchair accessible trails in Glacier National Park. It is a loop hike that begins and ends along the Going-To-The-Sun Road. It is a trail that is less than a mile long near Lake Mc Donald. It has great views of the tall cedar trees and abundant scenery.

Two Medicine is less visited than other parts of Glacier National Park. But it has fantastic views, rushing waterfalls, and reflective lakes. It has 4.5 miles roundtrip of hiking paths or you can view its fabulous scenery by taking a boat trip. At Two Medicine Lake, grab your binoculars and scan the steep mountain side to spot bighorn sheep, mountain goats, and possibly even a black or grizzly bear.

The hike to Virginia Falls in Glacier National Park begins from the St. Mary Falls shuttle stop. Hikers will also have the option of starting their hike from the St. Mary Falls Trailhead, located roughly one-quarter of a mile to the east of the shuttle stop. This 3.1-mile roundtrip trail is considered a moderately challenging route, it takes an average of 1-1/2 hours to complete.

The lower elevation sections of Going to the Sun Road remain open all year. Going to the Sun Road is about 50 miles long. It has scenic views and provides access to many locations and activities. You can take a guided tour on a shuttle bus, or you can drive the road yourself. If driving, the road yourself, it offers places to pull over and sightsee. Call before heading out. Some parts of the road are closed at certain times of the year.

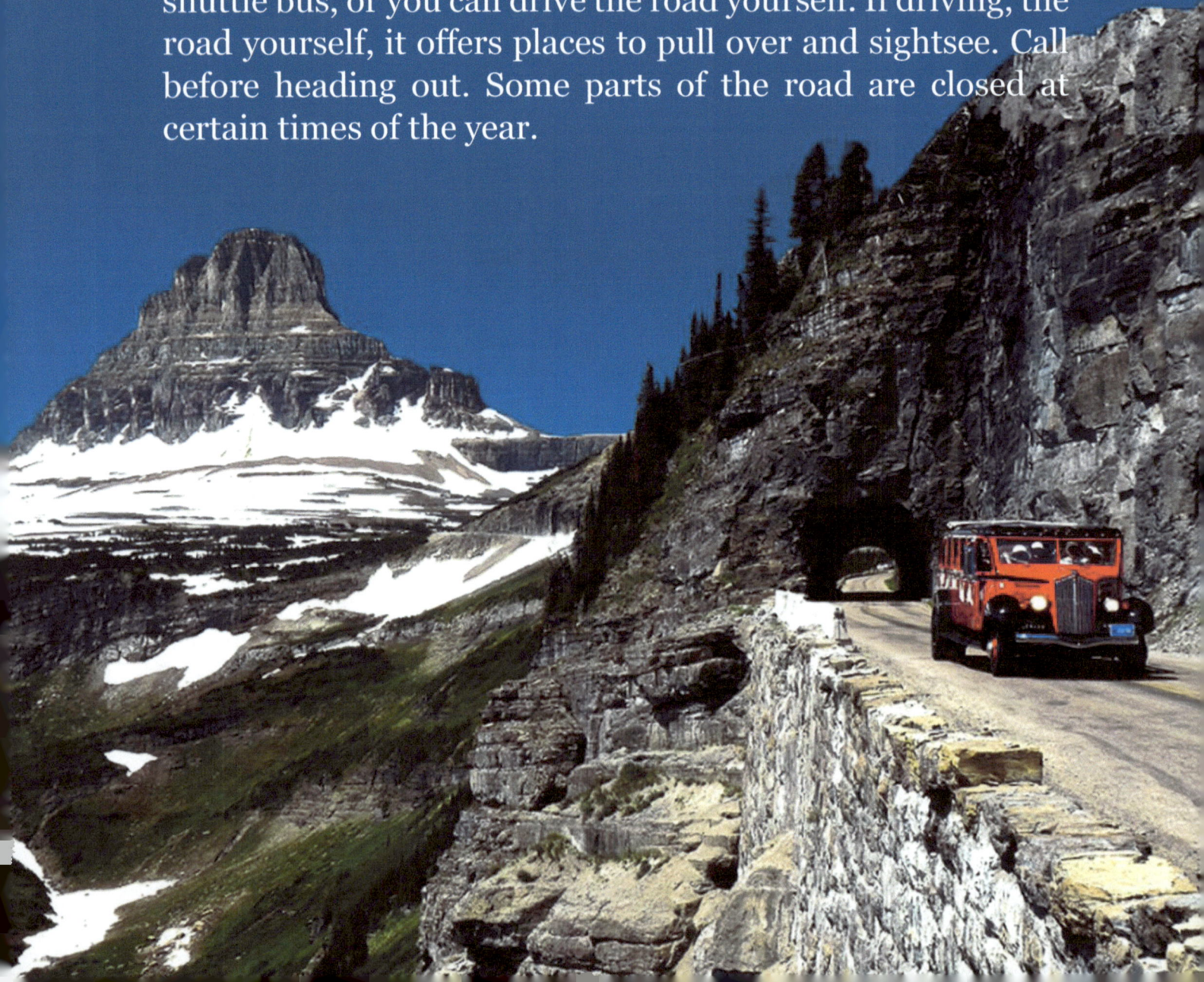

St Mary Lake and its mountains are located on the east side of Glacier National Park along the Going to the Sun Road. St Mary Lake is stunning. This lake is surrounded by huge mountains on three sides. Access to Saint Mary Lake is easy, the Going to the Sun Road follows the lake on its northern side. Numerous places along the road allow for an easy walk down to the lake.

If you don't feel like driving or hiking. You can take a shuttle or the red bus tour to view Glacier National Park. They have limited seating and are not open all year. Call ahead of time.

Facts About Glacier National Park

1. The best time to visit is June through October to avoid snow covered areas and slippery areas.

2. Awesome views of glaciers, mountains, waterfalls, rivers, streams, wilderness and animals.

3. Camping is allowed in most areas check before going.

4. Dogs are not allowed in most areas.

5. Mountain Goats are a symbol of the park.

6. Glacier National Park is located in northwest Montana.

7. The park covers more than 1 million acres, or around 1,580 square miles.

8. Going-to-the-Sun Road is one of Glacier Park's premier attractions.

9. Glacier National Park is home to. 26 glaciers, 175 mountains, 762 lakes, 200 waterfalls, 563 streams & rivers.

Author Page

Billy Grinslott & Kinsey Marie Books

ISBN - 9781960612939

Thanks